Max R. Spenser

# THE

# DIABETES

# FIX

## Natural Ways to Prevent and Reverse Type 2 Diabetes

# THE DIABETES FIX

# THE DIABETES FIX

# Table of Contents

# Introduction:

# What Is Diabetes?

Diabetes is a blood sugar disorder that comes in four different forms. Types 1 and 2 diabetes and gestational diabetes caused by high blood sugar levels are examples. High blood sugar levels cause gestational diabetes during pregnancy. Other types of the disorder cause genetic issues, and a malfunctioning pancreas causes other types.

Its symptoms include thirst and a frequent need to urinate. Both indicate that the kidney is not processing glucose, also known as blood sugar, in the person's body. The body reacts by attempting to eliminate excess glucose via frequent urination.

What's the reason? Our bodies cannot keep up with carbohydrate and sugar-heavy diets and sedentary lifestyles. This, in turn, leads to insulin resistance and a slew of other serious health problems.

Unfortunately, the standard type 1 diabetes treatment does not work for type 2 diabetes. If you have type 2 diabetes, there is plenty of evidence that insulin shots increase your risk of cardiovascular disease, stroke, and heart attack.

But there is a way out. Max R. Spenser, a natural health researcher and practitioner, demonstrates in The Diabetes Fix that dietary changes and intermittent fasting can help type 2 diabetes patients regain health while avoiding costly and invasive surgery.

However, to successfully heal your liver and kidneys and achieve your goal of treating type 2 diabetes, you must follow the instructions to prepare the daily morning cleanser for the liver and take the healing cleanser every day for 21 days.

No medication, but a proper diet and intermittent fasting are required.

Today, most medical professionals, including dietitians and diabetes specialists, regard type 2 diabetes as a chronic, progressive disease with no chance of parole. As natural health researcher and practitioner, Max R. Spenser demonstrates in this book.

Max R. Spenser, a natural health researcher and practitioner, explains how traditional therapies that rely on insulin or other blood-glucose-lowering medications can aggravate the condition by causing severe weight gain and even heart disease.

# THE DIABETES FIX

How to Reverse and Prevent Type 2 Diabetes

Nearly 400 million people worldwide have type 2 diabetes, with 28 million in the United States alone—and the number is growing.

Diabetes, particularly type 2 diabetes, is on the rise. One New York hospital recently reported treating ten times as many diabetes patients in 2000 as it had in 1990, with type 2 diabetes accounting for the vast majority of new cases.

# Chapter 1.

# What Is The Difference Between Type 1 And Type 2 Diabetes?

Your pancreas does not produce insulin in type 1 diabetes. It is the result of an autoimmune reaction.

The pancreas produces insulin in type 2 diabetes, but the cells do not respond to it as they should. This is known as insulin resistance.

Let's look at the distinctions between type 1 and type 2 diabetes.

**Diabetes Types 1 and 2:**

Diabetes is a problem that affects people of all ages. You've probably heard a lot about diabetes. Do you know the distinction between type 1 and type 2 diabetes? These two diseases have similar names, but they are not the same. These two have different reasons. Type 1 diabetes is generally more dangerous, and the risk is higher in younger people. Today we will discuss the differences and causes of these two types of diabetes.

**What exactly is type 1 diabetes?**

Immune system malfunctions cause medical documentation. The immune system of the human body defends us against harmful viruses and bacteria that enter from the outside, according to this theory about type 1 diabetes. This disease develops when the autoimmune response attacks our body's healthy cells. Because of this disease, insulin production in the body ceases, resulting in insufficient glucose reaching our cells. Insulin is essential for transporting glucose into cells.

Glucose serves as cellular fuel. When glucose does not reach the cells, the blood sugar level rises, and body function suffers. The condition can sometimes worsen. Dietary or lifestyle changes do not cause type 1 diabetes. The majority of the time, this is due to genetic factors. Currently, scientists are investigating why our bodies' immune systems are malfunctioning.

## What exactly is type 2 diabetes?

Insulin is produced in the bodies of type 2 diabetes patients, but it is not properly utilized due to resistance. In such cases, glucose accumulates in the bloodstream and becomes a source of disease. This can occur as a result of an unhealthy lifestyle and excess weight. Type 2 diabetes can also be passed down from generation to generation for genetic reasons. It harms how people's bodies function and causes problems.

# THE DIABETES FIX

The first is an autoimmune disorder. This means that the immune system of the body is attacking insulin-producing cells. Insulin is the hormone that regulates blood sugar levels.

Blood sugar levels rise when the body stops producing enough insulin. That is why type 1 diabetes patients require insulin shots to live safely.

Type 2 diabetes is distinct. It is usually the result of a poor, sugary diet. The body responds by producing large amounts of insulin to regulate all of the ingested sugar.

Insulin resistance develops in the body's cells over time. They no longer respond to insulin because too much of it is in the body.

As a result, insulin shots are not ideal for treating type 2 diabetes. After all, the problem isn't a lack of insulin, as in type 1 diabetes, but too much insulin.

## The Whole-Body Effect: How Type 2 Diabetes Affects Every Organ

Diabetes is a serious condition that can harm your eyes, heart, nerves, pancreas, lungs, sexual organs, and kidneys.

# THE DIABETES FIX

Understanding how diabetes affects your body is important. It can assist you in adhering to your treatment plan and remaining as healthy as possible.

The glucose in your blood rises if your diabetes is not well controlled. This is known as "hyperglycemia" (high blood sugar). High blood sugar levels can harm your body's very small blood vessels. Consider what happens to sugar when it is left unwrapped for an extended period. It becomes sticky. Consider how sugar "sticks" to your small blood vessels, making it difficult for blood to reach your organs. Blood vessel damage is most common in the eyes, heart, nerves, feet, and kidneys. Let's take a look at how this harm occurs.

**Eyes:** Long-term high sugar levels in the blood can harm the tiny blood vessels in the eyes. This can lead to vision issues or blindness. High glucose levels can cause retinal and blood vessel damage. The retina is a light-sensitive layer of tissue in the back of the eye. When this occurs, your body attempts to compensate by forming new, abnormal blood vessels much weaker and more prone to bleeding.

Other eye problems caused by diabetic retinopathy include:

# THE DIABETES FIX

**Diabetic macular edema (DME)**. It occurs when new, weaker blood vessels leak fluid and blood into the retina. This causes swelling of the macula, located in the retina's centre.

**Neovascular glaucoma**: This secondary glaucoma develops when new blood vessels form over the eye area where the cornea meets the iris. The cornea is the transparent tissue in front of your eye. The colored part of your eye is called the iris.

Seek medical attention immediately if you have diabetes and vision problems. Although these vision problems may be irreversible, treatment can prevent them from progressing to total blindness.

**The Heart:** The heart is the muscle that circulates blood throughout the body.

**Capillaries** are the smallest blood vessels in your body. They transport oxygen and nutrients throughout the body and waste products to the kidneys and liver. They also transport carbon dioxide to the lungs for exhalation.

**The Veins:** Your veins transport oxygen-depleted blood back to your heart.

# THE DIABETES FIX

Arteries transport oxygen-rich blood from the heart to the rest of the circulatory system.

High blood sugar levels can also harm your body's larger blood vessels, which supply oxygen to your heart and brain. Fat can also accumulate in blood vessels. This may result in a heart attack or stroke. According to the American Heart Association (CVD), diabetes is one of the seven major controllable risk factors for cardiovascular disease. Heart disease, stroke, and blood vessel disease are all examples of CVDs.

Coronary artery disease is the most common type of CVD (CAD).

It is caused by the buildup of plaque (cholesterol) in the artery walls. Diabetes increases your risk of coronary artery disease (CAD) by interfering with platelets, the cells that help your blood clot. Diabetes can cause plaques to form that are more prone to breaking off and blocking blood flow.

Over time, diabetes can also damage the blood vessels and nerves that control the heart. The longer you have diabetes, the more likely you are to develop heart disease.

**Nerves:** Nerves communicate vital information between your brain and the rest of your body.

# THE DIABETES FIX

Nerves function as conduits for electrical impulses between your brain and the rest of your body. These impulses assist you in feeling sensations and moving your muscles. They also perform autonomic functions such as breathing, sweating, and digestion. Neurons are another name for nerve cells.

High sugar levels in your blood for a long time can damage the blood vessels that bring oxygen to some nerves. Damaged nerves may cease to transmit pain signals.

Diabetes and the pancreas are inextricably linked. This is because your pancreas produces insulin. High blood sugar levels can occur when your pancreas fails to produce enough insulin.

This lack of insulin production causes type 1 diabetes. Type 2 diabetes, on the other hand, occurs when the body develops insulin resistance. This strains the pancreas as it attempts to produce more insulin than is required.

Most people with type 2 diabetes are more likely to develop pancreatic cancer, which can lead to diabetes development.

**Kidneys:** The kidneys are bean-shaped organs located beneath the rib cage and next to the spine. Each one is about the size of a fist. They are part of the renal system, which also includes the following:

# THE DIABETES FIX

Ureters are the tubes that transport urine from the kidneys to the bladder in our bodies. Urine is stored in the bladder until the kidneys expel it. The urethra is responsible for removing urine from the body.

The kidneys function as a filter system. They cleanse the body of waste, excess fluid, and acid. Healthy kidneys aid in the maintenance of a proper balance of water, salts, and minerals in the blood.

Consider your kidneys to be a coffee filter. They keep what you need inside your body while filtering out waste and excess fluid. Your kidneys are densely packed with blood vessels. High blood sugar levels can cause these blood vessels to narrow and clog over time. As your kidneys receive less blood, your body expels less waste and fluid.

The kidneys also produce vitamin D and erythropoietin. Vitamin D aids calcium absorption and promotes a healthy immune system. Erythropoietin is a hormone that stimulates red blood cell production.

# THE DIABETES FIX

Diabetes-related high blood sugar can damage the blood vessels in your kidneys over time. This can impair their ability to clean the body, resulting in waste and fluid buildup in the blood. Diabetes-related kidney disease is referred to as "diabetic kidney disease." Diabetic nephropathy is a type of kidney disease. In the United States, it is the leading cause of kidney failure.

If left untreated, diabetic nephropathy can lead to kidney failure, which can be fatal.

**Lungs:** Uncontrolled diabetes can impair lung function. This can result in minor complications such as asthma or more serious complications such as pulmonary fibrosis.

Researchers are baffled as to why people with diabetes can develop lung problems. Some believe that inflammation is the root cause.

Some research suggests that drugs used to treat low blood sugar may contribute to lung disease in diabetics. One study discovered that different medications could have different effects on the lungs. Glucophage (metformin), a common diabetes drug, is thought to protect against lung disease, whereas insulin may aggravate it.

**Sexual Organs:** Circulatory system damage reduces blood flow. This, along with nerve damage and the ability of nerves to send signals, can impair blood flow to the penis. In diabetic men, this can lead to erectile dysfunction.

The ability of your body to process glucose is also important for sperm health. When you have diabetes, you lose this ability, which can lead to poor sperm health. Mature sperm may be incapable of fertilizing an egg and may be less mobile.

Diabetes can also cause nerve damage in females, leading to vaginal dryness. Damage to blood vessels can also cause a lack of blood flow to the female reproductive organs.

Insulin aids in producing hormones that maintain reproductive tissues and regulate ovulation in females who do not have diabetes. When you have diabetes, this process is impaired.

The polycystic ovary syndrome has also been linked to diabetes (PCOS). High testosterone levels cause this condition. It can interfere with ovulation or egg release. This makes it difficult to conceive.

## How to Safeguard Your Organs

Develop a treatment plan with your healthcare team to help you manage your diabetes.

Exercise regularly.

If necessary, lose weight.

Consume healthy foods and stick to your diabetes meal plan.

Take all of your medications exactly as prescribed by your doctor.

Maintain regular eye examinations.

Get regular foot examinations. Wear shoes that fit properly and inspect your feet daily for injuries, blisters, or redness.

If you smoke, speak with your doctor about a quitting plan.

## Chapter 2

# Type 2 diabetes cannot be treated solely by restricting calorie intake.

Although it was initially proposed by doctors and nutritionists, a drastic reduction in daily calorie intake does not work.

But have you heard of Obediabetes? It's a new term, but it's a good way to describe a new trend in Western society: the epidemic of people suffering from obesity and type 2 diabetes.

Walter Willett, a nutritional expert at Harvard University, established the link between obesity and type 2 diabetes in 1990.

His research found that post-puberty weight gain is the most significant risk factor for type 2 diabetes. For example, putting on 44–77 pounds increases our chances of developing the disorder by an astounding 11,300%.

Willett and his colleagues conducted follow-up research in 1995. These studies found that even minor weight gain significantly increased the risk of developing type 2 diabetes. Adding a weight of 10 to 20 pounds increases the risk of type 2 diabetes by 90%.

Unfortunately, it took some time for these breakthroughs to be widely accepted in the medical community. However, there is no room for doubt today: type 2 diabetes is inextricably linked to weight gain and obesity.

However, neither obesity nor type 2 diabetes can be cured by simply cutting back on calories. When we eat fewer calories, our bodies lower their metabolic rates, which is the amount of energy required to keep our hearts pumping and our brains functioning.

Finally, our hunger and calorie intake are determined by our hormones. Our insulin levels, more specifically, are to blame. That means that the key to losing weight is to lower your insulin levels.

Reducing overall food consumption does not contribute to this goal. What we really need to do is avoid certain foods.

## 11 Diabetes-Resistant Foods and Drinks
Certain foods can raise blood sugar and insulin levels and promote inflammation, potentially increasing disease risk.

Carbohydrates have by far the greatest impact on your blood sugar, because they are broken down into sugar and glucose and absorbed into the bloodstream.

# THE DIABETES FIX

Carbohydrates are made up of starches, sugar, and fiber. Fiber, on the other hand, is not digested and is absorbed by your body in the same way as other carbs, so it does not raise your blood sugar.

Subtracting fiber from total carbs in a serving of food yields the digestible or net carb content. For example, a cup of mixed vegetables has 10 grams of carbs and 4 grams of fiber, so its net carb count is 6 grams.

When diabetics consume excessive carbohydrates at once, their blood sugar levels can reach dangerously high levels.

High levels can damage your body's nerves and blood vessels over time, potentially leading to heart disease, kidney disease, and other serious health problems.

Maintaining a low carbohydrate intake can help prevent blood sugar spikes and significantly reduce the risk of diabetes complications.

As a result, it is critical to avoid the following foods and beverages:

**Beverages with added sugar**:

Sugary beverages are the worst drinks to consume if you have diabetes.

# THE DIABETES FIX

For starters, a 12-ounce (354-mL) can of cola contains 38.5 grams of carbs.

The same amount of sweetened iced tea and lemonade contains nearly 45 grams of carbs derived entirely from sugar.

Furthermore, these drinks are high in fructose, linked to insulin resistance and diabetes. According to research, consuming sugar-sweetened beverages may, in fact, increase the risk of diabetes-related conditions such as fatty liver disease.

Furthermore, the high fructose content of sugary drinks may cause potentially harmful cholesterol, belly fat, and high triglycerides.

In another research studies in adults with overweight and obesity, consuming 25% of calories from high fructose beverages on a weight-maintenance diet resulted in increased insulin resistance and belly fat, a lower metabolic rate, and worse heart health markers.

Drink water, or unsweetened iced tea, club soda instead of sugary beverages to help control blood sugar levels and reduce disease risk.

**Trans Fats Are Synthesized Artificially.**

Trans fats made from chemicals are extremely harmful.

To make unsaturated fatty acids more stable, hydrogen is added to them.

Trans fats can be found in margarine, spreads, creamers, peanut butter, and frozen meals. Furthermore, food manufacturers frequently include them in crackers, muffins, and other baked goods to help extend the product's shelf life.

Although Trans fats do not directly raise blood sugar, they have been linked to increased inflammation, insulin resistance, belly fat, lower HDL (good) cholesterol levels, and impaired arterial function.

While more research is required to fully comprehend the connection between Trans fats and insulin resistance, the aforementioned associations are especially concerning for diabetics who are at an increased risk of heart disease.

Most countries have banned artificial Trans fats, and the Food and Drug Administration (FDA) banned the use of partially hydrogenated oil — the major source of artificial trans-fat in the food supply — in most processed foods in 2018.

This is not to suggest that all foods in the United States are now free of Trans fats. Trans fats are not required to be listed on nutrition facts labels if a product contains less than 0.5 grams of Trans fat per serving.

**White bread, brown rice, and spaghetti**:

White bread, rice, and pasta are processed carbohydrate foods.

It has been demonstrated that eating white bread, bagels, and other refined-flour foods significantly raises blood sugar levels in people with type 1 and 2 diabetes.

This reaction is not limited to products made with refined white flour. In one study, gluten-free pasta was also found to raise blood sugar levels, with rice-based varieties having the greatest effect.

Another study discovered that high-carbohydrate foods raised blood sugar levels and reduced brain function in people with type 2 diabetes and mental deficits.

These processed foods are low in fiber. Fiber slows sugar absorption into the bloodstream.

In other studies, replacing low-fiber foods with high-fibre foods was shown to significantly lower blood sugar levels in diabetics. Furthermore, people with diabetes had lower cholesterol levels.

fiber consumption improved the gut microbiota, which may have improved insulin resistance.

## Yoghurt with fruit flavors

Patients with diabetes may benefit from plain yoghurt. Fruit-flavored varieties, on the other hand, are a completely different story.

Flavored yogurts are typically made with nonfat or low-fat milk and are high in carbohydrates and sugar.

In fact, nearly 31 grams of sugar—or roughly 61% of the calories in a 1-cup (245-gram) serving of fruit-flavored yogurt—might be present.

Many people believe that frozen yogurt is a healthier alternative to ice cream. However, it can have just as much, if not more, sugar than ice cream (25Trusted Source, 26Trusted Source).

Rather than choosing high-sugar yoghurts, which can cause blood sugar and insulin spikes, choose plain, whole-milk yoghurt, which contains no sugar and may benefit your appetite, weight control, and gut health.

Fruit-flavored yogurts are typically low in fat but high in sugar, resulting in increased blood sugar and insulin levels. Plain, whole milk yogurt is healthier for diabetes management and overall health.

## Breakfast cereals with added sugar:

If you have diabetes, eating cereal can be one of the worst ways to start your day.

Despite the health claims on the packaging, most cereals are highly processed and contain far more carbohydrates than most people realize.

Furthermore, they contain very little protein, a nutrient that can help you feel full and satisfied while maintaining stable blood sugar levels throughout the day.

Even some "healthy" breakfast cereals are not suitable for diabetics.

For example, a 1/2-cup serving (about 56 grams) of granola contains 44 grams of carbs, whereas Grape Nuts contain 47 grams. Furthermore, each serves no more than 7 grams of protein.

Skip most cereals in favor of a protein-based low-carb breakfast to keep blood sugar and hunger under control.

# THE DIABETES FIX

Many breakfast portions of cereal have a high carbohydrate content but a low protein content. Breakfast with a high protein and low carbohydrate content is the best option for diabetes and appetite control.

## Coffee drinks with flavors:

A lower risk of diabetes has been associated with coffee consumption.

On the other hand, flavored coffee drinks should be considered a liquid dessert rather than a healthy beverage.

According to research, your brain does not similarly process liquid and solid foods. When you consume calories, you do not compensate by eating less lately, which may result in weight gain.

Carbohydrates are also abundant in flavored coffee drinks.

For example, a 16-ounce (473-mL) Caramel Frappuccino from Starbucks has 57 grams of carbs, while the same size as the Blonde Vanilla Latte has 30 grams of carbs.

Go for plain coffee or espresso with a tablespoon of heavy cream or half-and-half to keep your blood sugar under control and prevent weight gain.

# THE DIABETES FIX

Flavored coffee drinks contain a lot of liquid carbs, which can spike your blood sugar and leave you hungry.

**Maple syrup, honey, and agave nectar:**

Diabetics frequently try to limit their intake of white table sugar and treats such as candy, cookies, and pies.

On the other hand, other types of sugar can cause blood sugar spikes. In particular, brown sugar and "natural" sugars like honey, agave nectar, and maple syrup are examples.

Even though these sweeteners are not highly processed, they contain at least as many carbohydrates as white sugar. In fact, the majority of them contain even more.

The carb counts for a 1-tablespoon serving of the following popular sweeteners are listed below:

White sugar (12.6 g)

Honey 17.3 gram

16 grams of agave nectar

13.4 grams of maple syrup

# THE DIABETES FIX

According to one study, people with prediabetes experienced similar increases in blood sugar, insulin, and inflammatory markers whether they consumed 1.7 ounces (50 grams) of white sugar or honey.

Your best bet is to avoid all forms of sugar and instead use natural, low-carb sweeteners.

Although honey, agave nectar, and maple syrup are not as processed as white table sugar, they may have comparable effects on blood sugar, insulin, and inflammatory markers.

**Dried Fruits:**

Fruits contain various vitamins and minerals, including vitamin C and potassium.

When fruit is dried, water is lost, which results in even higher concentrations of these nutrients.

Unfortunately, it also becomes more concentrated in sugar.

Grapes have 27.3 grams of carbs, including 1.4 grams of fiber, in one cup (151 grams). In comparison, 1 cup (145 grams) of raisins has 115 grams of carbs, 5.4 of which are fiber.

As a result, raisins have more than four times the carbohydrate content of grapes. Other dried fruits are also higher in carbs than their fresh counterparts.

You don't have to give up fruit if you have diabetes. By sticking to low-sugar fruits, like fresh berries or a small apple, you can maintain healthy blood sugar levels and gain health benefits.

The sugar content of dried fruits increases, and they can contain up to four times as many carbohydrates as fresh fruit. For better blood sugar control, avoid dried fruit and choose low-sugar fruits.

**Snack foods in packages**

Snacking on pretzels, crackers, and other packaged foods is not a good idea.

They're typically made with refined flour and contain few nutrients, but they're high in fast-digesting carbs that can quickly raise blood sugar.

Following are some common snacks' carb counts for a 1-ounce (28-gram) serving:

Saltine crackers contain 20.7 grams of carbohydrates, including 0.78 grams of fiber.

# THE DIABETES FIX

Pretzels contain 22.5 grams of carbohydrates, including 0.95 grams of fiber.

Graham crackers contain 21.7 grams of carbohydrates, including 0.95 grams of fiber.

In actuality, some of these foods might have even more carbohydrates than what the nutrition label says. According to one study, snack foods contain 7.7% more carbs than the label claims.

If you get hungry between meals, eat nuts or a few low-carb vegetables with an ounce of cheese.

Packaged snacks are often highly processed foods made from refined flour, which can quickly raise blood sugar levels.

**Fruit Juice:**

Although fruit juice is a healthy beverage, its blood sugar effects are similar to sodas and other sugary drinks.

This applies to unsweetened 100% fruit juice and juice with added sugar. In some occasions, fruit juice contains more sugar and carbohydrates than soda.

For illustration, 8 ounces (250 mL) of soda and apple juice, respectively, have 22 and 24 grams of sugar in them. Grape juice contains 35 grams of sugar per serving.

Fruit juice, like sugar-sweetened beverages, is high in fructose. Fructose is responsible for insulin resistance, obesity, and heart disease.

A much better option is to drink water with a wedge of lemon, which contains less than 1 gram of carbs and is almost calorie-free.

Fruit juices have at least the same amount of sugar as sodas. But the high fructose content of these foods has been associated with insulin resistance, weight gain, and a higher risk of heart disease.

## Fries (French fries)

French fries are a food you should avoid, especially if you have diabetes.

Potatoes are relatively high in carbohydrates. 34.8 grams of carbohydrates—2.4 of which are fiber—make up one medium-sized potato.

# THE DIABETES FIX

However, once peeled and fried in vegetable oil, potatoes may do more than just raise blood sugar levels.

Deep-frying foods has been shown to produce toxic compounds such as AGEs and aldehydes. These compounds can cause inflammation and increase the risk of disease.

Several studies have linked a high intake of fries and fried foods to heart disease and cancer.

If you don't want to avoid potatoes, a small serving of sweet potatoes is your best bet.

Unhealthy oils, used to deep-fry french fries, may increase the risk of cancer and heart disease by promoting inflammation. They also contain a lot of carbohydrates, which raise blood sugar levels.

# Chapter 3.

## The role of insulin in energy storage

**What is insulin?  How does insulin cause fat storage?**

The pancreas produces and releases insulin into the blood, which is a hormone that the body produces to affect the functions of organs or tissues.

Food is broken down into essential nutrients when you eat (protein becomes amino acids, dietary fats become fatty acids, and carbohydrates become glucose), which then enter the bloodstream.

Insulin helps move the nutrients into cells by "ordering" the cells to open up and absorb them, which is then what is needed to transfer them from the circulation into muscle and fat cells for use or storage.

As a result, your pancreas releases insulin into the bloodstream each time you eat. Insulin levels gradually decrease as nutrients are gradually absorbed into cells, and once all of the nutrients have been digested, insulin levels eventually stabilize at a low, "baseline" level.

Every time you eat, a similar cycle takes place: after entering your bloodstream, amino acids, fatty acids, and/or glucose are joined by extra insulin, which then transports them to your cells. When the job is finished, insulin levels return to "normal," and the pancreas waits for us to eat again before starting the process all over again.

## Then what is the issue with insulin?

Insulin sounds like a decent dude when told. Without it, we would perish.

However, why do mainstream diet "gurus" attack it so harshly? Why do we hear that it makes us sluggish and ill?

Insulin prevents the breakdown of fat cells and boosts body fat production because one of its main functions in the body is to store fat. Insulin, in other words, tells the body to stop using its fat reserves and instead take some fatty acids and glucose from the blood, turning them into

more body fat. Because of this, it is typically demonized alongside the carbohydrate. This makes it an easy target and scapegoat. The "logic" works as follows:

Elevated-carb diets result in high insulin levels, which cause the body to store more fat and burn less fat over time.

# THE DIABETES FIX

## The corollary is as follows:

Low-carbohydrate diets result in low insulin levels, which increases fat burning and decreases fat storage, allowing you to maintain your weight loss.

These claims seem plausible at first look. Simple explanations are frequently used.

But they are based on false science and beliefs.

## Does Insulin Leads to Fat Storage?

It doesn't, however, make you fat. One of the common criticisms of carbohydrates and insulin is that if you eat a lot of carbohydrates consistently, your insulin levels will stay chronically high.

Your body will thus (supposedly) constantly be in "fat storage mode" and infrequently be in "fat burning mode," which results in weight gain.

While it's true that insulin makes it possible for fat cells to absorb fatty acids and glucose and so expand, this is not the actual reason why you gradually gain weight. It is overeating.

**Let's briefly look at how energy balance relates to fat gain and loss in case it doesn't make sense to you.**

Your daily energy expenditure and the amount of energy you provide your body through food constitute your energy balance.

You will gradually put on weight if you give your body a little more energy than it uses each day because some of the extra energy is stored as body fat.

If you give your body a little less energy than it uses each day, it will draw on its fat reserves to make up the difference, which causes you to lose weight gradually.

You see, your body needs a precise amount of glucose in the blood at any given time to keep you alive. Every cell in the body uses this essential fuel to function, and some organs, like the brain, are large glucose consumers.

When you eat, you provide your body with a sizable amount of energy (calories) in a brief length of time. When glucose levels rise far over what is required to sustain life, some of the excess energy is stored as body fat rather than being "thrown away" or used immediately.

According to science, your body is in the "postprandial" state when it is absorbing nutrients from food and storing fat (after meaning "after" and prandial meaning "having to do with a meal"). When the body is in "fat storage mode," it is said to be in a "fed" state.

The body enters the "post absorptive" state ("after absorption") once it has finished absorbing the glucose and other nutrients from the diet (amino acids and fatty acids), at which point it must turn to its fat reserves for energy. When you are "fasting," your body is in "fat burning mode."

Every day, your body alternates between being "fed" and "fasted," storing the fat from the food you eat and burning it after there is nothing more left over from the meals.

## Insulin-Facts:

In other words, you cannot lose weight unless you consume less energy than you burn. Likewise, you cannot gain weight unless you consume more energy than you burn.

No matter how many carbohydrates you eat or how high your insulin levels are throughout the day, this is the first law of thermodynamics in play. Neither fat stores nor energy limits may be increased or decreased in the absence of additional energy.

Those who despise carbs and insulin prefer to ignore the reality that dietary fat also suppresses HSL and that your body doesn't need much insulin to store dietary fat as body fat.

For this reason, consuming as much dietary fat as you like won't always lead to weight loss. And this is why research has shown that eating fats and carbohydrates separately has no effect on weight loss (eating carbs and fats combined has no impact either way).

Maintaining a good energy balance is key; if you constantly give your body more energy than it can use, whether in the form of protein, carbohydrates, or fat, you will gain weight.

More insulin may be released from meals with a high protein and low carbohydrate content than from meals with a high carbohydrate level. White bread in particular has been shown to be less insulinogenic than whey protein. The amount of insulin released is identical when eating brown rice or meat.

**Insulin works counter to how hunger is stimulated:**

Through scientific research, another common misconception has been disproven. Actually, research has shown that you feel fuller after a meal the more insulinogenic it is. Studies have shown that meals high in carbohydrates make people feel satiated for longer than meals high in fat, and this finding is consistent with those findings.

# THE DIABETES FIX

## Insulin Promotes Muscle Development:

Insulin has anti-catabolic properties, despite the fact that amino acids are unable to directly promote protein synthesis.

That suggests that when insulin levels are high, the rate of breakdown of muscle proteins slows down. This promotes a more anabolic environment where muscles can grow faster.

That makes logical, in theory, right? But does it work in clinical research? Yes, it does.

Numerous studies conclusively show that diets high in carbohydrates are preferable to those low in carbohydrates for increasing strength and muscle growth.

## What is the cause of Insulin Resistance?

If you are overweight and inactive, taking large amounts of carbohydrates on a regular basis will eventually cause problems. You'll develop a higher level of insulin resistance in your body, which could lead to Type 2 diabetes and make you more vulnerable to heart disease.

If you keep a healthy weight, exercise frequently, and eat at least a fairly reasonable diet, you'll never experience these problems. You won't lose your body's ability to use the carbohydrates you eat or its sensitivity to insulin.

# Chapter 4.

# Insulin Resistance: The overflow phenomenon

One of insulin's functions is to assist in the transport of glucose from the blood into the cells for energy. Insulin resistance occurs when blood glucose levels remain elevated despite normal or high insulin levels. Insulin's pleas for glucose absorption are being ignored by the cells. But why is this taking place? What factors contribute to insulin resistance?

The "lock and key" model is the current paradigm for understanding insulin resistance. The hormone insulin binds to a cell surface receptor to do its job. The insulin receptor functions as a lock, keeping the cell's gates shut. Insulin is analogous to the correct key. When inserted, the gate opens, allowing glucose from the blood to enter the cell and provide energy. When the key (insulin) is removed, the gate closes, and blood glucose can no longer enter the cell.

During the insulin resistance phenomenon, we imagine that the lock and key no longer fit together very well. The key (insulin) only partially and ineffectively opens the lock (receptor).

# THE DIABETES FIX

Because glucose cannot pass through the gate normally, less glucose enters the cell. Outside the gate, blood glucose builds up and becomes detectable as the clinical diagnosis of type 2 diabetes is made.

With less glucose inside, the cell is in a state of "internal starvation.' The body's first reaction is to produce more insulin. Because each key functions efficiently, the body compensates by producing additional keys. Yes, each key allows less glucose into the cell, but many of them exist.

**Additional keys:**  This hyperinsulinemia ensures that enough glucose enters the cells to meet their energy needs. A very interesting theory. Unfortunately, it has no basis in reality.

To begin, is the issue with the key (insulin) or the lock (insulin receptor)?

It is now relatively simple to determine the molecular structure of insulin and the insulin receptor.

When type 2 diabetic patients are compared to normal patients, it is clear that neither the insulin nor the receptor is defective.

THE DIABETES FIX

## So, what's the story?

If both the key and the lock appear normal, the only possibility is that something is clogging the mechanism. The lock and key interaction are hampered by some kind of blocker.

But what exactly?

This is where things get complicated. Various theories have been proposed to explain what prevents insulin from being released. We have no chance of treating insulin resistance unless we understand what causes it. When doctors and researchers have no idea what is going on, all the usual buzzwords come out. Inflammation, Oxidative Stress, the radicals.

While these may appear impressive, they simply reflect our ignorance and shed no light on the underlying cause of insulin resistance. These are all evasive responses.

Inflammation, like oxidative stress and free radicals, is a general response to injury.

Another pointer to a non-specific response to infection and injury is fever. Fever is a good indicator of infection. When we find a fever, we frequently find an underlying infection. The fever, however, did not cause the infection. Bacteria or viruses could be the root cause.

The same reasoning holds true for inflammation, oxidative stress, and free radicals. Something is causing injury, which

Causes inflammation, oxidative stress, and free radical formation, all of which are non-specific responses of the body.

The issue is whatever caused the injury, not the inflammation, oxidative stress, and inflammation, which are disease markers.

If, for example, inflammation were the root cause of heart disease, anti-inflammatory medications such as prednisone or non-steroidal anti-inflammatories would be effective in reducing heart disease. However, they are completely ineffective. They are only effective for diseases in which excessive inflammation is the root cause, such as asthma, rheumatoid arthritis, or lupus.

The same reasoning applies to oxidative stress, which is a marker of disease but not a cause. Oxidative stress is caused by an underlying injury that must be treated. This is why antioxidant therapy is so shockingly ineffective. When vitamin C, E, N-acetyl cysteine, and other antioxidant therapies are rigorously tested, they fail to prevent disease.

"Insulin resistance is caused by inflammation" is analogous to "gunshot wounds are caused by bleeding." It's useless. On the other hand, inflammation, bleeding, and fever are all useful indicators of disease and treatment efficacy. They indicate the presence of disease. If the fever subsides, the treatment (antibiotic) is likely to be effective. Inflammatory markers can also be used to assess treatment efficacy. If insulin therapy reduces inflammation, it is likely to be an effective treatment. Unfortunately, it does not.

We have no hope of properly treating insulin resistance unless we understand the underlying cause. The lock and key model with "internal starvation' is a nice story, but it cannot explain many of the type 2 diabetes phenomena. It falls short of explaining the central paradox of insulin resistance.

## The Central Illusion

Remember that when you eat, your insulin levels rise. Insulin primarily acts in the liver to aid in storing incoming food energy. Insulin instructs the liver to perform two functions.

1. Stop releasing new glucose from the body's stores.
2. To produce glycogen, switch to storage mode. When you're full, use De Novo Lipogenesis to make new fat (DNL).

Both actions of insulin should be blunted concurrently in a condition of high insulin resistance, such as type 2 diabetes.

This is certainly true for insulin's first action. Insulin tells the liver to stop producing new glucose, but the liver continues to do so. Glucose leaks into the bloodstream, causing the body to increase insulin levels.

The second insulin action should be blunted in an insulin-resistant state, but it is paradoxically enhanced. The insulin-resistant liver blocks glucose from passing through the gate using the outdated lock and key paradigm, causing "internal starvation." In this case, the liver cannot produce new fat, and DNL should be turned off. However, DNL not only continues but actually increases. So insulin's effect is accelerated rather than blunted!

Indeed, there is so much new fat being produced that there is nowhere for it to go. This causes an abnormal fat accumulation inside the liver, where there should be none. The amount of fat in the liver should be low, not high. However, type 2 diabetes is strongly linked to excessive fat accumulation in the liver.

How does the liver resist one of insulin's effects while accelerating the other? This occurs in the same cell, in response to the same insulin levels, and with the same insulin receptor. This makes no sense at all. Insulin sensitivity is reduced and increased simultaneously and in the same location!

Despite many decades of research and millions of dollars, the world's top researchers were all perplexed by the central paradox of insulin resistance. There were research papers written. Various hypotheses were proposed, but they all failed because the old "lock and key" paradigm of insulin resistance and internal starvation was incorrect. The underlying premise of

# THE DIABETES FIX

Type 2 diabetes treatment disintegrated like a house built on a crumbling foundation.

## How can we account for this apparent contradiction?

The crucial hint is that insulin causes insulin resistance. The primary issue is hyperinsulinemia, not insulin resistance.

When it is more difficult to transport glucose into the cell for a specific amount of insulin, this condition is known as insulin resistance. Then, however, this does not necessarily imply that the gate is stuck. Other factors contribute to glucose's inability to enter that resistant cell. Perhaps the glucose cannot enter the cell because it is already full.

## The new paradigm of insulin resistance as an overflow phenomenon resolves the central Illusion.

This changes everything. If you believe in the old 'lock and key/internal cellular starvation' model, then the proper treatment is to increase insulin as much as necessary to push that pesky glucose into the cell.

For the past 50 years, we have treated type 2 diabetes in this manner. And it's been a complete failure. The failure of this paradigm was demonstrated by the randomized controlled trials ACCORD/ADVANCE/VADT/TECOS/SAVIOR/ORIGIN.

# THE DIABETES FIX

If the 'overflow' paradigm is correct, increasing insulin to push more glucose into an overflowing cell is EXACTLY wrong! This would exacerbate diabetes. Which is EXACTLY what we see in the clinic.

Patients with type 2 diabetes do not improve as we prescribe insulin; instead, they deteriorate. Their blood glucose levels are better, but they gain weight and develop all complications — heart disease, stroke, kidney disease, blindness, and so on.

The correct treatment for the overflow paradigm is to empty the body of excess glucose, not just the blood.

**How?**

Low carbohydrate, high-fat diets and intermittent fasting can both help to reduce the underlying cause of hyperinsulinemia.

**What's more, guess what?**

That is EXACTLY what we see in the clinic. When we begin fasting for type 2 diabetes patients, they lose weight, their medication requirements decrease, and the cycle eventually reverses.

# THE DIABETES FIX

**In Summary: Liver fat deposits are the cause of Insulin resistance and can progress quickly.**

Most people are aware that excessive alcohol consumption is detrimental to the liver. However, alcohol is not the only cause of liver damage.

Let's start with glycogen, a substance in our bodies that stores carbohydrates. Too much of it causes fatty liver deposits, leading to insulin resistance over time.

Insulin resistance is the first step toward developing type 2 diabetes. It is caused by an excess of carbohydrate and protein consumption.

In contrast to other dietary fats, which can be stored throughout the body, glucose from protein and carbohydrates is transported directly to the liver. When it arrives, it is converted into a glycogen reserve that can be used when blood sugar levels fall.

However, once this reserve is depleted, the body begins converting new glycogen into fat, which is then exported to other body parts.

The issues arise when the liver cannot keep up with protein and carbohydrate intake. As a result, the liver begins to store the fat since it can no longer be exported. And as the liver fattens, it stops accepting new glucose.

# THE DIABETES FIX

Insulin is released when our blood sugar levels rise. As a result, the liver is encouraged to accept more glucose. More insulin is released to correct the problem when the liver struggles to process the glucose.

This results in a vicious cycle. The greater the amount of insulin in our bodies, the less the liver reacts to it. That is what doctors mean when they speak of insulin resistance.

And developing a fatty, insulin-resistant liver is not difficult.

# Chapter 5

# Rising Fructose Consumption Contributes To The Prevalence Of Fatty Liver Disease.

Endocrinologist Robert Lustig released a video to YouTube in 2009 that quickly went viral. In it, he validated what many people had thought for a long time: sugar is poisonous to the body.

One sort of sugar is very damaging to our health. It's called fructose, and it plays a crucial role in the development of type 2 diabetes.

Fructose, like glucose, is harmful and devoid of nutritional value, especially in processed versions. It does, however, have an additional sting in its tail: the liver cannot break it down.

Because roughly 80% of glucose is processed outside the liver, the organ only has to cope with one-fifth of all ingested glucose. Fructose, on the other hand, is easily absorbed by the liver, where it can cause fatty liver disease and, eventually, diabetes.

This is because the liver simply cannot digest huge amounts of fructose on top of the glucose it already receives from proteins and carbs.

# THE DIABETES FIX

The bad news is that fructose is now more ubiquitous in our diets than ever before.

That is the issue: fructose isn't intrinsically bad for humans; what affects our health is consuming too much of it.

People ingested roughly 15-20 grams of fructose per day in the nineteenth century, largely in the form of fresh fruits containing relatively tiny levels of the sugar.

However, following WWII, people's diets began to shift. This was mostly due to increased production of sugar cane and sugar beets. By the 1970s, the average daily fructose consumption per person had climbed to 37 grams.

The advent of fructose-rich corn syrup, on the other hand, was the most devastating development. It was a cheap supply of sugar, and it was rapidly introduced to a variety of processed meals. It was eventually found in everything from sauces to ready meals, breads, and sweets.

By 2000, per capita fructose consumption in the United States had climbed to 78 grams per day. There is no doubt that this contributes to the situation.

According to the author's own research, countries where corn syrup is popular have 20% more incidences of diabetes than countries where less fructose is consumed.

## Metabolic Syndrome: What Is It?

What precisely is metabolic syndrome?

"Metabolic syndrome" is a set of risk factors for heart disease that raise your chances of having heart disease, stroke, and diabetes. Other names for the illness include Syndrome X, insulin resistance syndrome, and dysmetabolic syndrome. A national health survey indicated that more than one in every five Americans has metabolic syndrome. The prevalence of metabolic syndrome climbs with age, with more than 40% of those in their 60s and 70s affected.

## Who is prone to metabolic syndrome?

People suffering from central obesity (abdominal/waist fat accumulation)

People who have diabetes or a strong family history of diabetes.

People who have other clinical indicators of "insulin resistance," such as acanthosis nigricans ("darkened skin" on the back of the neck or underarms) or skin tags (typically on the neck), should visit a doctor.

Certain ethnic groups are more likely to have metabolic syndrome.

# THE DIABETES FIX

As you become older, your chances of developing metabolic syndrome rise.

## What variables contribute to metabolic syndrome?

It is uncertain what causes metabolic syndrome. Many features of the metabolic syndrome are linked to "insulin resistance." Insulin resistance develops when the body's use of insulin to decrease glucose and lipid levels is ineffective. Insulin resistance may be caused by a combination of hereditary and environmental factors. Dietary choices, physical activity, and possibly disrupted sleep patterns are examples of lifestyle factors (such as sleep apnea) (such as sleep apnea).

## What symptoms are present in metabolic syndrome?

Usually, there are no apparent physical symptoms right away. Medical complications related to the metabolic syndrome emerge gradually. Consult your doctor if you are unsure whether you have metabolic syndrome. He or she will be able to make the diagnosis after obtaining the relevant tests, which include blood pressure, lipid profile (triglycerides and HDL), and blood glucose.

## How is the metabolic syndrome identified?

If you have three or more of the following symptoms, you have metabolic syndrome.

A waistline of at least 40 inches for men and 35 inches for women (measured across the belly) (measured across the belly).

If you have a blood pressure of 130/85 mm Hg or above, or if you use blood pressure medication,

A triglyceride level greater than 150 mg/dl is

A fasting blood glucose (sugar) level of more than 100 mg/dl or if you are on glucose-lowering medication.

A normal high-density lipoprotein (HDL) level is less than 40 mg/dl in men and 50 mg/dl in women.

## What can you do to avoid or reverse metabolic syndrome?

Because physical inactivity and excess weight are the primary underlying contributors to the development of metabolic syndrome, exercising, eating healthy, and attempting to lose weight if you are currently overweight or obese can help reduce or prevent the complications associated with this condition. to help you manage some of the symptoms of metabolic syndrome. Some techniques for minimizing your risk include:

# THE DIABETES FIX

Healthy eating and weight loss if you are currently overweight or obese: Healthy nutrition and moderate weight loss (5% to 10% of body weight) will help restore your body's ability to recognize insulin and considerably enhance your wellbeing.

This minimizes the probability of the syndrome evolving into a more serious illness. This can be accomplished through diet, exercise, or, if prescribed by your doctor, weight-loss medications.

Increased activity can improve insulin sensitivity on its own. Aerobic activity, such as a 30-minute daily walk, can help you lose weight, improve your blood pressure and lipid levels, and lessen your chance of getting diabetes. Most doctors prescribe 150 minutes of aerobic exercise per week. Even if no weight is lost, exercise may reduce the risk of heart disease. Even if you can't get in 150 minutes of exercise per week, any increase in physical activity is beneficial.

**Changes in diet:** Maintain a diet in which carbohydrates account for no more than 50% of total calories. Carbohydrates should be obtained from whole grains (complex carbohydrates), such as whole grain bread (rather than white bread) and brown rice (instead of white). Whole grain products, along with legumes (such as beans), fruits, and vegetables, provide more dietary fiber. Reduce your consumption of red meat and poultry. Eat more fish instead (without the skin and not fried) (without the skin and not fried). Fat should account for 30% of your daily calories. Healthy fats, such as those found in canola oil, olive oil, flaxseed oil, and tree nuts, should be consumed.

**What health issues could arise if you have metabolic syndrome?**

High levels of insulin and glucose are linked to a variety of negative changes in the body, including:

Damage to the lining of the coronary and other arteries, a precursor to heart disease or stroke,

Changes in the kidney's ability to remove salt result in hypertension, heart disease, and stroke

Triglyceride levels rise, increasing the risk of developing cardiovascular disease.

An increased risk of blood clot formation can cause artery blockage, heart attacks, and strokes.

A decrease in insulin production can indicate the onset of type 2 diabetes, a disease associated with an increased risk of heart attack or stroke, uncontrolled diabetes is also linked to eye, nerve, and kidney complications.

Fatty liver is sometimes associated with liver inflammation (non-alcoholic steatohepatitis, or NASH); if left untreated, NASH can progress to cirrhosis and liver failure.

## Chapter 6

## What to Do If You Have Type 2 Diabetes

**Insulin administration is not the answer to diabetes treatment.**

Undoubtedly, the ability to produce insulin in laboratories and treat type 1 diabetes was a significant medical breakthrough. However, insulin shots are not a cure-all in the fight against type 2 diabetes.

Type 2 diabetes and obesity are more than just health concerns. If they aren't treated, they can cause heart attacks and other cardiovascular diseases.

Insulin shots aren't very effective in that situation. Although they can aid type 2 diabetes patients in controlling their blood sugar levels in the short term, they can be detrimental to their health over time. They might even play a role in a person's premature death in some circumstances.

G.L. Duff and G.C. MacMillan demonstrated this in 1949. Their animal studies revealed that high insulin levels could cause atherosclerosis or artery hardening linked to heart attacks and strokes.

# THE DIABETES FIX

Modern research also shows that insulin shots are ineffective for treating type 2 diabetes. They consistently show that lowering blood sugar levels raises the risk of heart disease.

Consider the ACCORD study from the American National Institute of Health, which examined whether insulin treatment could reduce cardiovascular deaths in type 2 diabetes patients.

One group of patients received standard insulin doses and heart medication. The other group received higher insulin and heart medication doses. The goal was to lower the blood sugar levels of the second group faster.

The study was a colossal failure. Patients who received higher insulin and medication doses died 22% sooner than those who received standard doses. Finally, the entire study had to be canceled.

Another study was conducted in 2010 by J.M. Gamble, a Canadian scientist. He discovered that type 2 diabetes patients receiving insulin treatments were 279 percent more likely to develop the coronary disease than other patients.

**Although bariatric surgery can be an effective treatment for type 2 diabetes, it is not the best solution**.

Obesity is a serious issue. Consider one of the author's patients, Adrian, who weighs 208 kilograms and lost his job due to his health problems.

# THE DIABETES FIX

Many patients in similar circumstances consider a drastic solution: elective weight loss surgery.

The procedure is called bariatric surgery, which entails removing a large portion of the stomach.

It is an effective treatment for type 2 diabetes; in most cases, the condition disappears after the procedure.

So, how exactly does it work?

The operation, on the other hand, drastically reduces the number of calories that can be consumed. It enables the liver to burn off the fatty deposits that have made it insulin resistant and all of the glycogen previously stored in the liver.

P.R. Schauer and his colleagues demonstrated the effectiveness of the surgery in a study conducted at the Cleveland Clinic in 2012.

Patients with type 2 diabetes who underwent bariatric surgery had significantly better health than those who received insulin treatments. After three months, the former patients could discontinue their diabetes medication completely—they were all cured!

Ninety-five percent of type 2 diabetes patients who undergo the procedure may experience this. Long-term weight loss and lower blood pressure are also advantages of bariatric surgery for more than 70% of all patients.

So that must be the cure for everything?

# THE DIABETES FIX

No, it does not. The problem is that the procedure is extremely expensive, highly invasive, and can result in a slew of complications down the road. Internal bleeding, infection, and decreased nutrient absorption are examples.

However, there is a silver lining. The good news is that much less invasive methods can achieve the impressive results of invasive bariatric surgery. We'll take a look at them in the next few seconds.

Avoiding fructose and refined carbohydrates can prevent and reverse type 2 diabetes.

A three-year-old type 2 diabetes patient was admitted to a Texas hospital in 2015, making him the youngest diabetes patient ever.

That's a good indication that the disorder has gotten out of hand, and understanding how to prevent and reverse type 2 diabetes is more important than ever.

So, how can it be reversed and avoided? You can implement two highly effective strategies right now.

**The first is to stay away from fructose**.

The most obvious place to begin is to eliminate sugar from your kitchen and dining table. That includes sucrose (a sugar made up of one part glucose and one part fructose) and high-fructose corn syrup.

When you eliminate fructose from your diet, you must be cautious about the products that contain it. Sweet drinks such as cocktails, smoothies, and flavored waters fall into this category.

Candy, cakes, and pastries are not permitted. However, keep in mind that bread and pasta frequently contain added sugar. Check the ingredients list and leave any sugar-containing items on the supermarket shelf.

Use caution when it comes to sauces, condiments, and even meats. Sugar is a simple way to make any food taste better.

Vendors and producers are aware of it, which is why they include it in their products.

Eating out can be a minefield, especially if you do it frequently. Before placing your order, don't be afraid to ask your waiter about the fructose content of various dishes.

**Avoiding refined carbohydrates is the second strategy you can use to prevent and reverse type 2 diabetes.**

Refined carbohydrates are the worst food group because they cause your insulin levels to skyrocket. Avoid refined wheat-based products such as bread, pasta, corn tortillas, popcorn, fries, chips, and white rice.

That doesn't mean you should abandon old favorites. Not all carbohydrates are bad for you; switch to unrefined carbs like brown rice and whole-wheat pasta to keep eating your favorite foods.

These alternatives, which do not stimulate insulin production nearly as much as their refined counterparts, can be included in a healthy diet.

Removing refined carbohydrates from your diet leaves a gap in your nutritional strategy. Fill it with healthy fats like high-quality oils, fish, avocados, and nuts.

## Chapter 7

## Natural Methods for Preventing and Reversing Type 2 Diabetes

**The effectiveness of intermittent fasting and ketogenic diets in treating type 2 diabetes.**

Diabetes has long been known to be cured by fasting. In 1916, Elliott Joslin, an early American diabetes specialist, advocated for it as a treatment.

However, much has changed in the medical field since then. Today, the emphasis is increasingly shifting toward using drugs to treat diabetes. However, it is time to re-discover more traditional treatments.

**So, what is fasting all about?**

Daily portion control is one option, but it's probably not the best solution. Curing diabetes and encouraging weight loss are not easy tasks.

Consider a 2015 British study that examined the effectiveness of traditional nutritional counseling that focused on portion control and concluded that this approach failed 99.5 percent of all participants. They did not lose much weight.

It doesn't work because lowering your daily calorie intake slows your metabolic rate while increasing your hunger sensation. That is difficult to bear, and most dieters eventually give up and return to their original weight.

## Intermittent fasting is a far superior strategy:

That means abstaining from all foods for a set period, ranging from a day to a week. People can then resume their normal diets.

Following this plan requires much more concentrated effort, making it easier to implement than the daily grind of portion control.

Most importantly, it functions! Fasting causes a decrease in insulin production, which means the body remains insulin-sensitive rather than developing resistance to the hormone.

Another British study, conducted in 2011 by N.M. Harvie demonstrates the efficacy of this approach. Harvie compared two diet groups. The first followed a Mediterranean diet with calorie restrictions, while the second normally ate five days a week and fasted the other two.

# THE DIABETES FIX

Both groups lost weight after six months, but the second had significantly lower insulin levels than the first.

This suggests intermittent fasting may be the most effective treatment for type 2 diabetes. After all, the disorder is caused by high insulin levels and insulin resistance, which fasting helps to reduce.

## The Benefits of Liver Detox:

### How to Effectively Treat and Reverse Type 2 Diabetes in 21 Days

Daily Liver Cleansing in the Morning

Contains enough for one serving, which may be consumed daily for 21 days.

teaspoon lime juice

teaspoon of apple cider vinegar.

tsp. pure honey

quarter teaspoon of turmeric

Cayenne pepper, 1/8 teaspoon

quarter teaspoon of rosemary

In an 8-ounce glass of warm water, combine all ingredients and drink.

# THE DIABETES FIX

## Why is this detox necessary?

There are numerous types of cleansers and detoxifiers available.
Some of these are pre-mixed and ready-to-use. They can be very
expensive, and determining why this is so can be difficult.
Spices can be pricey, but each glass contains only one-fourth of
a teaspoon of spices. The cost is most likely due to the ease of
not having to measure and mix.

The benefit of this detox, as well as measuring and mixing it
yourself, is that you know exactly what you're eating and why
the ingredients are beneficial, specifically for declogging your
liver's filtering system and keeping it running as an efficient
glucose warehouse and manufacturing site.

## Lemon juice:

Limes are citrus fruits that contain various limonoids, which are
phytochemicals. Phytochemicals are plant-derived substances
that work in our bodies to protect us from disease and prevent
cell damage. These limonoids help the liver enzyme glutathione-
S-transferase (GST).

Toxins are neutralized and removed from your body by GST.

Lime juice also aids in the opening and clearing of the bile
ducts.

# THE DIABETES FIX

## ACV (apple cider vinegar):

Other products can be used to make vinegar, but apple cider vinegar is the most common.

It is particularly beneficial to the liver. It is produced by using bacteria and yeast to convert sugar into acetic acid.

Acetic acid is responsible for the sour taste of vinegar. Apple cider vinegar promotes glycogen storage in the liver.

Apple cider vinegar is also useful around the house. It's an excellent, environmentally friendly product for cleaning and disinfecting the kitchen and bathroom. Use it to clean windows, wipe down counters and tiled surfaces, and mop up spills.

## Honey:

Honey has been extensively researched, and it has been established that it aids in preventing liver damage caused by obstruction. It's been used for years with lemon to relieve coughs and make thick mucus in the throat easier to get rid of, and it's also been used to treat allergies and hay fever.

## Turmeric:

This is a plant that is commonly used to flavor curry dishes. Curcumin, its main component, gives it a beautiful bright yellow color. Indian and Chinese healers have used turmeric for centuries due to its anti-inflammatory properties. According to recent research, turmeric may help improve the liver's ability to filter and detoxify harmful substances in the blood by increasing GST, the liver enzyme that neutralizes and eliminates toxins

## Chili pepper

Capsicum is a plant. This plant's fruit is a red chili pepper used to make capsaicin.

Capsaicin, the component that gives cayenne pepper its spicy flavor, is also a medicine. Cayenne pepper is used by

It has been used for thousands of years by Native Americans to treat gastrointestinal disorders, and it is also used in traditional Japanese and Chinese medicine and Indian Ayurvedic therapies.

## Rosemary:

Rosemary is a plant that can be grown almost anywhere on the planet. It grows best in warm, sunny climates. It's used as a seasoning in foods and beverages, particularly in Mediterranean cuisine, and it has a wonderful stress-relieving scent in soaps and lotions.

## Warm water:

Warm or room temperature water is ideal for detox.

## This is why:

Some of the enzymes in lime juice and the other ingredients in the detox mixture may be destroyed by boiling water, making their healing and cleansing properties less effective. Consuming

# THE DIABETES FIX

he detox ingredients in or with ice cold water may reduce their absorption. When served cold, the detox takes longer and requires more effort to absorb.

Water is essential for everyone's survival, but it is especially critical during healing. When it comes to diabetes treatment, water quality is even more important. Water accounts for more han 70% of your body weight. To help flush the accumulated oxins out of your liver and out of your body, drink 10 glasses of water per day. If the water you drink contains contaminants, it ncreases your kidney and liver workload. Not all water available for purchase is the same.

## The timing of detoxification:

For best results, detoxing should be done first thing in the morning, roughly 30 minutes prior to breakfast. This is because healing ingredients are more quickly absorbed when introduced nto your system on an empty stomach. The detox also acts as a digestive aid and can improve your stomach and intestinal health, helping your liver rejuvenate and your liver and kidneys get rid of toxins more effectively.

On the other hand, the daily morning cleanser for the liver is not optional. To be successful and achieve your goal of curing your diabetes, you must drink the healing cleanse every day for 21 days in a row.

## THE DIABETES FIX

Food is more thoroughly digested, waste and toxins are more efficiently eliminated, and your body is nourished and revitalized.

# THE DIABETES FIX

## Disclaimer

All contents in this book is created and published for informational purposes only. It is not intended to be a substitute for professional medical advice and should not be relied on as health or personal advice.

Always seek the guidance of your doctor or other qualified health professional with any questions you may have regarding your health or a medical condition.

Made in United States
Troutdale, OR
11/24/2024

25267510R00040